J   Beatty
641.59
BEA

Food and recipes of Mexico

DATE DUE			

Kids in the Kitchen™
The Library of Multicultural Cooking

Food and Recipes of Mexico

by Theresa M. Beatty

The Rosen Publishing Group's
PowerKids Press™
New York

The recipes in this book are intended for a child to make together with an adult.
Many thanks to Ruth Rosen and her test kitchen!

Published in 1999 by The Rosen Publishing Group, Inc.
29 East 21st Street, New York, NY 10010

First Edition

Book Design: Resa Listort

Photo Credits and Photo Illustrations: Cover photo by John Bentham; p. 5 © 1995 PhotoDisc Inc.; p. 6 by Ira Fox; pp. 7, 9, 17 by Christine Innamorato; pp. 8, 14, 16 © John Novajosky; pp. 10, 13, 21 © George Ancona/International Stock; p. 15 © Pablo Maldonado; p. 18 © Michele and Tom Grimm/International Stock.

Beatty, Theresa M.
  Food and Recipes of Mexico / by Theresa M. Beatty.
    p.   cm. — (Kids in the kitchen : multicultural cooking)
  Includes index.
  Summary: Describes some of the foods that are eaten in Mexico and includes recipes for several popular dishes.
  ISBN 0-8239-5224-X
  1. Cookery, Mexican—Juvenile literature. 2. Food habits—Mexico—Juvenile literature. [1. Food habits—Mexico.   2. Cookery—Mexican] I. Title. II. Series: Beatty, Theresa M. Kids in the kitchen.
TX716.M4B36 1998
641.59`72—dc21   98-11776
                                                                    CIP
                                                                    AC

Manufactured in the United States of America

Contents

Abbreviations

cup = c.   Farenheit = F.   tablespoon = tbsp.   teaspoon = tsp.

Celsius = C.   kilogram = kilo   liter = l   milliliter = ml

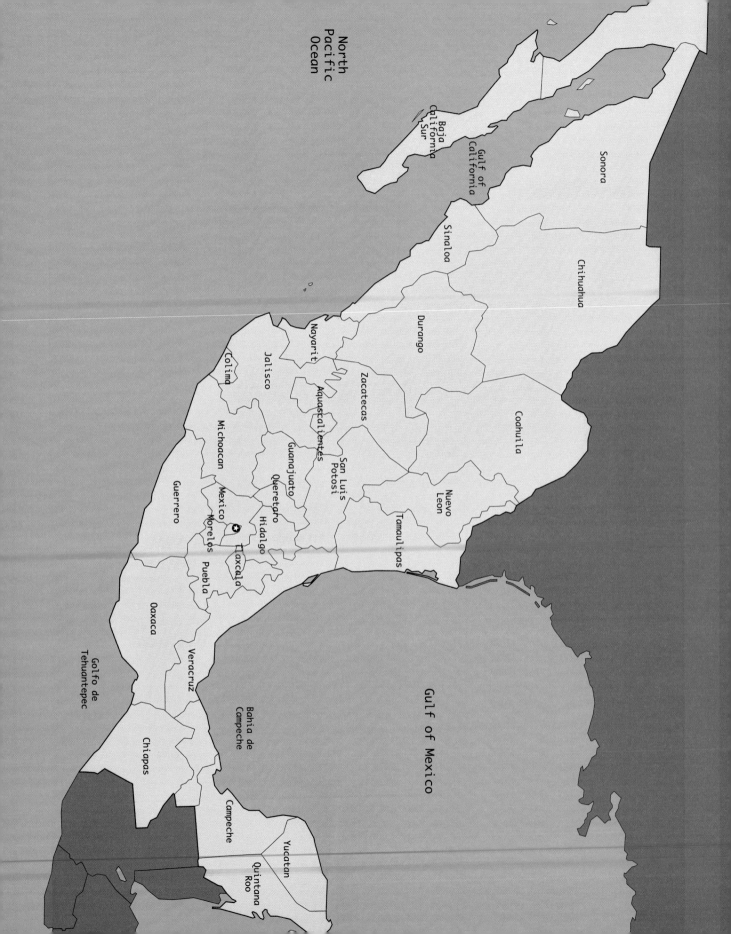

North
Pacific
Ocean

Baja
California
Sur

Gulf of
California

Sonora

Sinaloa

Chihuahua

Nayarit

Durango

Colima

Jalisco

Zacatecas

Aguascalientes

Coahuila

Michoacan

Guanajuato

San Luis
Potosi

Guerrero

Queretaro

Nuevo
Leon

Mexico

Hidalgo

Morelos

Tlaxcala

Tamaulipas

Puebla

Oaxaca

Golfo de
Tehuantepec

Veracruz

Bahia de
Campeche

Gulf of Mexico

Chiapas

Campeche

Yucatan

Quintana
Roo

Mexico

Mexico is located in the southern part of North America. The lands of Mexico change from **tropical** (TRAH-pih-kul) forests in the south to rocky mountains in the north and west.

Many of the foods used in modern Mexican cooking have been grown throughout Mexico for thousands of years. The ancient Maya of southern Mexico and Central America, who were most powerful during 250 and 900 AD, and the Aztecs of Central Mexico, who ruled from the 14th to the 16th centuries, both grew corn and chilies. These foods are still very important to Mexican cooking today.

▶ *More than 90 million people live in Mexico.*

European Influence

In the 1500s Spanish **conquistadors** (kon-KEES-tuh-dorz) from Europe arrived in the land that is now Mexico. The **native** (NAY-tiv) people living there grew food that the Europeans had never seen or tasted. Tomatoes, corn, beans, and sweet potatoes were all new to the Spanish. They traded foods with one another. When the Spanish sailed back to Europe, they took Mexican foods with them. The new foods quickly became important in Spanish and other European cooking.

The trading worked both ways. Europeans brought animals that the native peoples in Mexico had never seen, such as cows, pigs, sheep, and goats. At the time, these were unknown in North America.

Nachos

You will need:

1 c. *(250 ml)* tomatoes, finely chopped

1 green pepper, seeded and sliced

2 jalapeno peppers, diced

½ c. *(125 ml)* chopped scallions

2 c. *(500 ml)* grated Monterey Jack cheese

1 12 oz. *(.30 kilo)* bag tortilla chips

guacamole

salsa

sour cream

HOW TO DO IT:

Preheat oven to 350 degrees F. *(175 degrees C.)*.

In bowl, mix tomatoes, peppers, and scallions.

Place layer of chips on a baking sheet covered with foil.

Sprinkle tomato mixture evenly over chips.

Sprinkle cheese on top, covering most of the chips.

Bake for 10 minutes, or until cheese has melted.

Serve on a large tray with guacamole, salsa, or sour cream for dipping.

Always ask a grown-up to help you when using knives!
Always ask a grown-up to help you when using the stove or oven!

Tortillas

Tortillas (tor-TEE-yuhz) have been a **staple** (STAY-pul) of the Mexican diet for thousands of years. In many parts of Mexico, a meal without tortillas is not complete.

Tortillas are made from corn or flour. Corn tortillas are made by grinding corn and water together on a hard surface to make a dough called *masa*. This thick dough is rolled into flat, thin cakes and cooked on a griddle over a fire. Flour tortillas are made by mixing flour and water together and rolling the dough into thin, round cakes. The cakes are then baked in an oven.

Tortillas can be eaten in many ways. Often, they are filled with cheese, beans, or meat to make tasty tacos or burritos.

Chicken Enchiladas

You will need:

- 8-10 large flour tortillas
- 2 c. *(500 ml)* chicken, cooked and shredded
- 2 tbsp. *(30 ml)* olive or vegetable oil
- ½ c. *(125 ml)* chopped scallions
- 1 medium onion, chopped
- 1 green pepper, seeded and sliced
- ½ cup *(125 ml)* fresh cilantro or 1 tbsp. *(15 ml)* dried cilantro
- 1 jalapeno pepper, sliced
- ½ tsp. *(2 ml)* salt
- ¼ tsp. *(1 ml)* black pepper
- 1 clove garlic, minced
- 1 3 oz. *(.125 kilo)* can tomato paste
- 3 tomatoes, finely chopped
- 1 c. *(250 ml)* shredded Monterey Jack cheese

HOW TO DO IT:

- In a medium-sized saucepan, heat oil. Preheat oven to 350 degrees F. *(175 degrees C)*.
- Place scallions, onion, pepper, and jalapeno pepper in the saucepan and cook over medium heat for 2 or 3 minutes.
- Add tomatoes, chicken, garlic, cilantro, salt, and pepper. Cook for 5 minutes, stirring often.
- Stir in tomato paste and cook for another 10 minutes. Then lower heat and simmer for 15 minutes.
- Remove pan from heat and lay one tortilla flat on a plate.
- Spoon ½ to ¾ cup of the chicken mixture onto tortilla.
- Roll up the tortilla and place seam-side down in a greased baking or casserole dish. Repeat until you run out of tortillas or mixture.
- Bake for 15 minutes.
- Pull out dish and sprinkle cheese over enchiladas.
- Bake for another 10 minutes, or until the cheese is melted.

Serves 8-10

Always ask a grown-up to help you when using knives!
Always ask a grown-up to help you when using the stove or oven!

Foods of Mexico

Beans, corn, chilies, avocados, and sweet potatoes are staples of Mexican **cuisine** (kwih-ZEEN). Tomatoes are very important too.

Cilantro (sih-LAHN-troh) is an herb used in many Mexican recipes. It looks a bit like parsley and was brought to Mexico by the Spanish.

Corn is a common food in Mexico. There are many ways of preparing corn. There's even a Mexican drink made from corn. **Atole** (ah-TOH-lay) is a corn drink made from boiled *masa* and water. Sometimes people add cinnamon or sugar to this drink, which is kind of like a thick milk shake.

▼ *Mexican people often dry their own herbs and peppers.*

Mealtime

In some parts of Mexico, people eat as many as five meals a day. People who lead a **traditional** (truh-DIH-shuh-nul) Mexican way of life eat an early breakfast and a brunch around eleven in the morning. Then they will eat the **comida** (koh-MEE-dah) at two or three in the afternoon, a small snack around seven in the evening, and a light supper before they go to sleep.

One reason for eating five meals a day is so families can spend a lot of time together.

In large Mexican cities, most people eat just three meals a day, like people in many other countries.

In Mexico, food is more than a way to fill up an empty stomach. Meals are meant to be shared and enjoyed with family and friends.

La Comida

The comida is the main meal of the day. It often lasts for two or three hours. The comida is eaten during the hottest part of the day.

Businesses close during this time so that everyone can go home and have a long, relaxing meal with their families. The meal includes soup, such as *caldo de camaron*, or shrimp soup, rice and beans, and a main dish, such as *pollo en salsa verde*, or chicken in green sauce. Vegetables, such as *calabacitas al vapor*, or steamed squash, are part of the meal also. A dessert, such as *cocada horneada*, a baked dish of coconut, eggs, raisins, and sugar, finishes the meal.

Sopa de Arroz
(Rice Soup)

You will need:

2 tbsp. (30 ml) vegetable oil

⅔ c. (150 ml) cooked rice

1 clove garlic, crushed

1 medium onion, chopped

1 green chili pepper, chopped

3 tomatoes, chopped

4 c. (1 l) beef or chicken stock

1½ tsp. (7 ml) salt

HOW TO DO IT:

Heat oil in saucepan over medium heat.

Add rice, garlic, onion, and chili pepper. Fry until brown, stirring often.

Add tomatoes, stock, and salt.

Simmer for 20 minutes. Serve hot.

Serves 4

Always ask a grown-up to help you when using knives!
Always ask a grown-up to help you when using the stove or oven!

Sauces

Sauces add flavor and color to many Mexican meals.

Guacamole (gwah-kuh-MOH-lee) is a creamy sauce made from mashed avocados. Mexican cooks use guacamole to flavor many dishes. This bright green sauce can also be served as a dip for tortilla chips.

Salsa (SAHL-sah) is often served in Mexico and in Mexican restaurants all over the world. It is a mixture of onions, tomatoes, cilantro, and chilies. Salsa can be made very spicy by adding lots of chilies.

Salsa

You will need:

- 2 tbsp. *(30 ml)* olive oil
- ½ small onion, finely chopped
- ⅓ cup *(75 ml)* fresh cilantro, chopped or 1 tbsp. *(15 ml)* dried cilantro
- 2 medium tomatoes, finely chopped
- ½ tsp. *(2 ml)* oregano
- 2 garlic cloves, minced
- 2 tsp. *(10 ml)* red wine vinegar
- ½ tsp. *(2 ml)* salt

HOW TO DO IT:

- In a medium-sized frying pan, heat olive oil over medium-high heat.
- Add onions and garlic. Cook until they are clear, about 2 to 3 minutes
- Remove from heat. Add the rest of the ingredients and mix well. It's okay to mash up the tomatoes.
- Cool for 3 hours.
- Serve with tortilla chips.

Always ask a grown-up to help you when using knives!
Always ask a grown-up to help you when using the stove or oven!

Local Cooking

As in every country in the world, there are many different styles of Mexican cooking. Different kinds of foods, or ingredients, are found in certain areas of the country, so styles won't be the same from city to city.

The southern city of Veracruz lies right next to the Gulf of Mexico. Fish is very popular there. A spicy shellfish soup called **chilpachole** (cheel-pah-CHOH-leh) is a well-known dish in Veracruz.

People in the Yucatan peninsula make sauces from fruit instead of chilies or other vegetables. **Papa-dzules** (pah-pah-DZOOL-ayz) are common in the Yucatan. They are tacos filled with hard-boiled eggs and a squash-seed sauce.

The people of the Chinchorro Banks fishing village in Chetumal, Mexico, have a diet that includes plenty of the fish they catch in the Caribbean Sea.

Desserts

One of the most popular desserts is a type of custard called **flan** (FLAHN). Hot chocolate is another popular treat in Mexico. Did you know that Europeans never tasted chocolate until the conquistadors brought it back from Mexico?

Sweets are often served during **celebrations** (seh-luh-BRAY-shunz) such as the **Dia de los muertos** (DEE-uh day lohs MWER-tohs), or the Day of the Dead. It takes place during the first two days of November. Dia de los muertos is a way for people to remember, with happiness, the lives of friends and family members who have died. Special candies shaped like skulls and coffins are eaten in honor of this occasion.

This scary skull is actually a sweet treat! ▼

Mexican Food
Around the World

Have you ever heard of Tex-Mex or Southwestern cooking? These are styles of cooking based on Mexican cuisine. Tex-Mex cooking is a blend of Mexican cooking and foods from the state of Texas in the United States. Chili con carne is a stew that was created using the flavors of Mexico. It is made from beans, chilies, and meat.

Tortilla chips, refried beans, burritos, and tacos are popular in many places. These and other foods from Mexico are served at restaurants and sold at stores all over the world.

You can prepare and serve a little bit of the flavor of Mexico for your friends and family with the recipes in this book. *Buen provecho*, or enjoy!

Glossary

atole (ah-TOH-lay) A drink made from corn.

celebration (seh-luh-BRAY-shun) A special time honoring something or someone.

chilpachole (cheel-pah-CHOH-leh) A spicy shellfish soup.

cilantro (sih-LAHN-troh) An herb used in many Mexican dishes.

comida (koh-MEE-dah) The main meal of the day.

conquistador (kon-KEES-tuh-dor) A Spanish explorer of Mexico in the 1500s.

cuisine (kwih-ZEEN) A style of cooking.

Día de los muertos (DEE-uh day lohs MWER-tohs) The Day of the Dead; a time when the lives of family and friends who have died are remembered.

flan (FLAHN) A custard dessert.

guacamole (gwah-kuh-MOH-lee) A sauce made from mashed avocados.

native (NAY-tiv) From a certain area.

papa-dzules (pah-pah-DZOOL-ayz) Tacos filled with hard-boiled eggs and a squash-seed sauce.

salsa (SAHL-sah) A sauce made with cilantro, chilies, onions, and tomatoes.

staple (STAY-pul) A very important and basic food item.

tortilla (tor-TEE-yuh) A flat bread made from corn or flour.

traditional (truh-DIH-shuh-nul) A way of doing something that is passed down through the years.

tropical (TRAH-pih-kul) Very hot and humid.

Index